Other Titles by *Langaa* RPCIG

Francis B Nyamnjoh
Stories from Abakwa
Mind Searching
The Disillusioned African
The Convert
Souls Forgotten

Dibussi Tande
No Turning Back. Poems of Freedom

Kangsen Feka Wakai
Fragmented Melodies

Ntemfac Ofege
Namondo. Child of the Water Spirits

Emmanuel Fru Doh
Not Yet Damascus
The Fire Within

Thomas Jing
Tale of an African Woman

Peter Wuteh Vakunta
Grassfields Stories from Cameroon

Ba'bila Mutia
Coils of Mortal Flesh

Kehbuma Langmia
Titabet and The Takumbeng

Ngessimo Mathe Mutaka
Building Capacity: Using TEFL and African languages as development-oriented literacy tools

Sammy Oke Akombi
The Raped Amulet
The Woman Who Ate Python & Other Stories

Susan Nkwentie Nde
Precipice

Milton Krieger
Cameroon's Social Democratic Front: Its History and Prospects as an Opposition Political party, 1990-2011

Francis B Nyamnjoh & Richard Fonteh Akum
The Cameroon GCE Crisis: A Test of Anglophone Solidarity

Their Champagne Party Will End!

Poems in Honor of Bate Besong

Editors
Joyce Ashuntantang & Dibussi Tande

***Langaa* Research & Publishing CIG**
Mankon, Bamenda

Bate Besong
(May 8, 1954 – March 8, 2007)

Publisher:
Langaa RPCIG
(*Langaa* Research & Publishing Common Initiative Group)
P.O. Box 902 Mankon
Bamenda
North West Province
Cameroon
Langaagrp@gmail.com
www.langaapublisher.com

ISBN: 9956-558-19-2

DISCLAIMER
All views expressed in this publication are those of the author and do not necessarily reflect the views of Langaa RPCIG.

Indeed, they have sworn fealty to their masonic lodges
& to each other to bankrupt our national coffers
The curse on the heads of the corrupt banditti.
There is evidence that evil still survives absolutely
And the only good is a cripple, chained to the dungeon of
Mockery and dust.
But their champagne party will end...

Bate Besong, "Their Champagne Party Will End"

Contents

Foreword

News of the deadly road accident that terminated Bate Besong's earthly life in the early hours of dawn on March 8th 2007 sent shock waves around the world. In one stroke of the road, as it were, Anglophone Cameroon had lost its foremost fiery writer and fearless social critic. Admired by the cross section of an oppressed and subjugated Anglophone minority in Cameroon who saw him as the torchbearer of truth, Bate Besong was scorned by the regime in power that cringed every time he appeared on TV or spoke over the radio. Indeed his vitriolic pen had exposed Cameroon for what it is—a benevolent dictatorship with copious social aberrations and political abnormalities masquerading as a democracy.

Born on May 8, 1954, Bate Besong attended the Hope Waddell Training Institute in Calabar and the St. Bede's Secondary School in Ashing, Kom in Cameroon, from where he left to do a BA in Literary Studies at the University of Calabar. It was in Calabar that Besong founded *Oracle*, the first Nigerian university journal of poetry edited by students. Just before he graduated from the University of Calabar, Besong published his widely acclaimed maiden collection of poems, *Polyphemus Detainee & Other Skulls*, that was launched by Chinua Achebe. Upon his graduation from the University of Calabar in 1980, Besong did his National Youth Corps training in Nigeria before enrolling at the University of Ibadan for an MA degree.

Realizing that his emerging reputation as a budding writer was gradually giving him recognition as a Nigerian and compromising his Cameroonian nationality, Bate Besong opted to return to Cameroon after completing his MA in Ibadan. To his utter dismay and much in despair, he was viewed in Cameroon with suspicion and mistrust. In utter desperation, he took up a teaching job at the Cameroon Protestant College in Bali where he taught from 1983 to 1985. It was in Bali that he met and got married to Christina, his life-long spouse and friend who gave meaning to his convoluted life and shielded him from the slings and arrows of a home country that neither recognised his talents nor appreciated his artistic vision. Eventually he was recruited in the Ministry of Education in 1985. Without a salary for more than four years, his integration file kept on disappearing every time he re-submitted it to the Ministry. Because of this persecution he went into depression and began drinking and smoking profusely.

Paradoxically it was during this period of depression, extreme poverty, and despair that he became quite prolific and wrote some of his most provocative works: *The Most Cruel Death of the Talkative Zombie, Obansinjom Warrior With Poems After Detention, Requiem for the Last Kaiser*, and *The Banquet*. Partly because of his critical writings and his militant activism during the Ahidjo era, he was punitively transferred to the North of Cameroon where his depression deepened and he almost took away his own life. Fortunately, he was transferred to Buea, the unofficial capital of Anglophone Cameroon. Yet this did not stop his tense encounters with the Cameroon government.

The staging of Besong's *Beasts of No Nation* on March 26, 1991 at the University of Yaoundé Amphi 700 brought him into a head-on collision with Cameroon's belligerent regime. Shortly after the play was staged, Besong was kidnapped during a broadcast visit to the State television house. State security agents, who took him to an unknown location, physically assaulted and tortured him. Within a few minutes, news of his kidnapping was broadcast around the world. Embarrassed by the kidnap news, state security agents released Bate Besong as quickly as they had kidnapped him. To this day, no explanation was provided by the ruling regime as to why he was kidnapped or who masterminded the kidnapping.

In the early hours of March 8, 2007, Bate Besong's epic battle with the system came to a fiery end when he was killed in a ghastly accident on the infamous Douala - Yaounde highway. The previous evening of March 7 2007, Besong's last book, *Disgrace* - a collection of poems – had been launched at the University of Buea. Unbeknownst to all those who gathered for this grandiose ceremony, it was Besong's very public farewell party to friends, family and fans... The last poem in the collection, "The night is over..." is hauntingly prophetic:

> O! after so much crush of stamens
> In the brain:
> Whose chilling whirrs, sought
> A dwelling shroud in the next plane
> I have passed this way, gathering
> In the angsts

And in the last stanza of "The night is over..." Besong evokes this chilling, prophetic imagery:

A hooded shuttle amidst showering
Sparks.
But oh! Alas
The night has sunk level with the earth
Gradually, it lowers out of sight. Dawn!
The nightly round of our esoteria is over...
Did Bate Besong foresee his earthly demise together with the other
two men of letters who died with him (Gwangwa'a and Ambe)?
Perhaps. We shall never know. Suffice it to say that Bate Besong
(the man) fondly nicknamed BB (the poet/dramatist) died like he
lived: in a bang and live theatrical embellishment—dawn, blood,
mangled metal, and decapitated cadavers—just like "The night is
over ..." prophesizes—with sparks!

As the gory details of the road accident that claimed his
life unfolded in the early hours of March 8, on the Douala-
Yaounde highway, Cameroon woke up to the implication of his
tragic death. The annoying gadfly that the experiment called
Cameroon always tried to brush off its shoulder, but who was
consistently around the corner compelling the nation to confront
its own inhumanity, was no more.

The outpouring of grief, anger, bewilderment, protest,
incomprehension, denial, and yes, conspiracy theories about his
death, worldwide, was spontaneous and overwhelming. The
selected poems you are about to read attempt to capture some of
the angst that we all felt when the news reached us in the early
hours of dawn, that fateful day on March 8, 2007. They try to put
into perspective the essence of that Anglophone Cameroon literary
icon, the fearless Obasinjom warrior with the bemused smile, who
once upon a time, was called Bate Besong.

Ba'bila Mutia,
Yaoundé, Cameroon
January 2008

Tributes in Verse

A Tribute To Bate Besong, the Fallen Hero
Sarah Anyang

BB! I call you "EKINNI ACWHINGBE"-
The crying voice of the Ngbe Cult.

So your last outing

Was yesterday?

Your book launch

was your final exit!

Indeed a small soldier ant

has bitten my mouth,

Ayo me! Death indeed is a thief!

May you step on feaces and not on thorns.

"Ekinni", Neko piti piti!!!

Morgantown Failed
Joyce Ashuntantang

BB, I had planned the celebration
I had called all friends
BB, I had planned it all
The *Banquet: a historical Drama*
Obasinjom warrior in town
The writer as tiger in glory.
I was ready for the story…
Once Upon Great Lepers...
Morgantown 2007
BB, I said "At last"
ALA will see your face
I said "At last"
The name behind the cryptic words revealed.
I said "At last"
we'll flaunt you in "our" world
Basking in delayed sunshine.
Morgantown 2007
Yes, was not to be
You turned it to a Requiem
A Requiem for the last Kaiser
Our literary Kaiser.
I still hold your other grain
"The grain of Bobe Jua"
Your second poetic foray
This was '86
I read your hand
"to a fine actress" you wrote
And the ink stayed wet
Drying up yesterday in *Disgrace*
But this exit BB, remains untimely
All the plans, all the hopes
We are left suddenly like *Beasts of No Nation*.
Like Change Waka and His man Sawa Boy
You dragged Ambe and Ni Tom for the ride
To *The Most cruel Death*…
BB, *Up above Cameroon*
You have gone but you remain our giant
One eye giant in the land of the blind
Seeing *The polyphemus Detainee and other skulls*
So we chant and continue to gnash our teeth

Yes, Morgantown failed
But I'll be there BB
The party will hold, a teary banquet,
with swollen eyes and hushed voices.
For collective grief
Our catharsis.
Sleep well, Be well.

* The author was to meet Bate Besong at the African Literature Conference (ALA) held at West Virginia University, Morgantown, from 14-18 March 2007. However BB died on his way to pick up his visa at the American embassy in Yaounde. This poem is a celebration of BB's life and creative works which appear in italics.

The Mountain Weeps
Ilongo Fritz Ngale

The mourning seems to have no end
As the morning star of joy seems to have fled,
For the mountain bleeds
Its flanks red with blood
Which copiously flows through the pores of its kids,
Poor souls taken off into tragedy lane
Slain before their time

As UB weeps.
Psychic mines waylay life
Blowing minds and bodies to shreds tragic
Rocking the boat of existence through tragedy bouts,
Raising vapours of fear and superstition
In the night of the night,
Time when demons walk
Walking like men during the day
But really half devils and half beasts in their subtle bodies unseen,
Roaring in blood-lust
Ready to devour more innocents
Even as UB weeps.
Come the unending funerals
The hypocrites grimace in macabre crying fake,
But really trying hard not to laugh at fallen heroes
Now laid flat on their backs,
No longer able to conjugate verbs and spray bullets of light
At ghost masters and regents of dooms-day kingdom,
Seeming to reign for now
As UB weeps
And all barely whisper: "Who is next?"
Is this the end then?
God forbid, for only one side of the story has been told,
The other being the legendary half man, and half rock
Womb for slowly bubbling magma
That will soon flow as invincible fire,
And woe betide the evil ones
For the blood-stained psychic courtyards
Polluted by black magic will be burned to stubble
Bringing to ashes the heathen priests who invoke the abyss.
The giants are gone, yes
Slain by the angels of chaos,

And the tender shoots are woebegone for a while,
But these will soon stand on gigantic shoulders
To take the weeping people forward into mutation vales
As they tread on the serpent in pain
Smashed to pieces by fire from the rock,
And peace once more descends onto death-scorched hearts and land
The hearth of regeneration bursting forth into rays of hope,
That will blind the usurpers,
As UB once more sups with its children
On bread of love.

The Ghost of Um Nyobe
(Musings from the Other Side of the Bridge)
Dibussi Tande

They say you died in enemy territory
They say you died on the wrong side of THE BRIDGE
But what better place to die
- On the other side of the bridge -
Than in the Sanaga Maritime -
The sacred land of the *Ngog Lituba*
The springboard of Cameroun nationalism
The heartland of the Cameroun resistance;
Purified with the blood of thousands of patriots
Who said NO! to the imperialists and neo-colonialists?

You met your maker at Misole II
Down the road from Boumnyebel -
Birth place of Ruben Um Nyobe
The venerated *Mpodol*
The immortal soul of the *gwet bi kundè*
who is entombed in hallowed ground
in Eseka – still farther down road…
Surely his spirit watched over you
At that fateful moment
Gently guiding you towards your seat
On the pantheon of departed heroes
Where you rightly belong

The sleepy hamlet of Misole II
Is now etched in our collective consciousness
Not as a symbol of death and despair
Not as a symbol of dreams unfulfilled
But as a reminder of battles past
Of battles lost - of battles won
Of battles yet to come;
And a rallying cry
To the Obasinjom Warriors
Who shall restore this land
To its erstwhile glory

The Flight of Poet-Eagles
Mukwelle Akale

The summons of the gentle voice of the Great Muse,
Descends at dawn as minds of mere mortals ponder repose,
Striking the hearts and minds of the few
eagles of mortals that pay heed....
With bewildering passion they feed
On the dew of timeless essences of the beauty
and refinement of the language of the gods,
It is they the poet-eagles who absorb into their systems,
the inexhaustible ambrosia-nic flavour of the mighty in verse and
language.
So Homer, Byron, Keats, Okigbo and now Bate Besong,
Stood strong and tall,
Piercing the ever dark clouds of hopelessness throughout time,
Armed with courage and fearless drive,
Empowered by the gods with the power of the clarion call,
Charge through the frighteningly monstrous clouds of despair,
While puny mortals wait lamentably for the ever elusive dissipation of
the dark clouds...
And now, with their sudden flight, we see the silver lining.

Unrepentant Intellectual
Valentine Gana

Tragedy strikes at the break of dawn
As the window of death
Cracks an opening at the sight of life
And makes a widow of our nursed hopes

Death; an assured thief that steals indiscriminately
With a method that promises notice to no one
And reserves tomorrow to neither you, nor I
Sorrow abounds in the hearts of fans
In the soul of brothers and comrades
As sadness looms over a people
Drowned by a legendary loss

Death; enough of your dreadful deeds,
Pirate of our loved ones, Unwelcome visitor
Give us a break;
The time for your vacation is past due
For you took Besong, Gwangwa'a, Ambe
Who never belonged to your merciless hands
The writer as a tiger said his thunderous last
Unbeknownst to him, as he set his sights
To where only eagles dare to dream

Bate Besong; Writer, Critic, Dramatist
Or if you prefer, Unrepentant Intellectual
BB; Orator, Poet, Patriot, Philosopher
As were his comrades, ambushed by death

Leaving us at a loss for words
Adios to a towering mind
Who insisted on staying as a gift
Who never stopped giving
To the world of critical thinkers
And true to his calling,
Died with the brethren of his craft

When will the howls of the afterlife
Cease to dial
With a tone, that makes an illusion of life
In its snatching away of such formidable men

With such refined minds
That turned life's perplexing challenges
Into the mirror of a dramatical illusion

Dreadful Women's Day!
(To The Obasinjom Warrior)
Fr Tatah H. Mbuy

Death, wither do you come, whither do you go,
That on your trail you have the audacity
To shake the Mighty Literary Iroko?
Death, wither comes this gut that you dare
Into our Academic Shrine to ruffle
The Dreaded, moon-headed Obasinjom Warrior?
Your Showmanship certainly wins no approval,
Being only an ugly, sloven display.
Death, wither do you come, wither do you go,
That midstream you have the tenacity
To engage the ferocious shark bare-handed ?
Death, wither comes this stoicism that you sneak
Into the Temple of Causation, seeing no Effect
And wrestle with the Academic Totem, coming out victorious?
Your characters are Corinthian, all in bad shape,
Their Performance only amateurish, though lethal.
I think I hear the wise Seneca speak:
Death respects neither age nor rank,
Being only an ill-bred diplomat, bad at negotiations.
Death appears callous to the health
Being only an obstacle to they that need time.
Blissful it is to they that suffer incurably;
Sublime to those that have lived to the full;
Merciful to they that seek assisted suicide.

Non Comprehendo! Why B.B ?
Why this Obasinjom Literary Warrior:
Ready to rattle any words for the voiceless?
Mentor of the rustic; charm of the scholar,
Dread of political lilliputs; scarecrow to con-men.
Bate, why this mortal crescendo before the denouément?
Why this resignation after a night charged with Art?
Why this dance of a coward in mid-challenge?

 I think, I hear Bate Speak:
I bow out of a stage I thought I owned,
And kiss this earth from which I was made,
Not in Cowardice but to dine with our Literary Gurus:
Ben Fonlon, Ken Saro-Wiwa; Kitts Okigbo, Malcom X;

William Dubois, Cheikh Anta Diop!
Could anyone resist the invitation to such a party?
Not B.B.! Accuser of the Last Kaiser!

Comprehendo! O wise one!
What a literary party up there!
All noble minds fed with no filth;
No bribe possible for Admission,
No rituals, no pretence in that Temple.
Every discussion puts the "jokers" all on the Table,
Merit counts!
All argue with a logic more coherent than Aristotle's;
All end with a wisdom more serene than Sophocle's.
Comprehendo B.B. Farewell brother;
But keep the ink flowing from the Eternal Academia.
Requiescat In Pace.

In the Hot Wastes
Alfred Kisubi

In the hot wastes of home,
Village and town huddle
In tsunami hailstorm
Life,
A small niggard,
Clutches his dribble,
Death,
An incessant wind
At every window
Even cactus
Lies dormant in the desert,
Deep in the dusty loam
Seeds of sanity now dormant
Wait to grow and ripen,
When new rains pour -
To quench miserable goats,
Browsing on roots of grass
We give them dry cactus

Warrior Falls at the Warfront
Christopher Fon Achobang

Hail Bate Besong, the Obasinjom Warrior,
You went to the warfront,
Chasing vampirish necromancers,
You took Ambe, you met an army of Beasts,
Those of no Nation, and said,
Enough to their soulless plunder of the Nation.
Locust that rented havoc on the green notes, CFA,
In plane loads they were flown to Europe
And your people chaffed and died of hunger.

Hail Bate Besong, you took your war to the Zombies,
The talkative Zombies; they laid in wait for you,
Posthumous Professors, Comatose Professors,
Kabukabu lecturers.
Your fiends were replete, both,
In the Place To Be and Came roes.
Like the prawns of Mabeta,
Your foes waited for your warship to be wrecked

I thought you always had the shield of Nyangkpe,
Behold your ship was wrecked and your head,
Sliced with blunt savage razors for Mbongo Chobi.
Your blood, Ambe's and Kwasen's,
Became ingredients for musong portions of Edea.

They believe you are dead.

BB, you live on in your trilogies, verses and students.
I take your mantle; I pick your hat from your blood,
I seize it and place on my head as armour,
I move to the warfront to avenge your slaying.
The vampirish necromancers, blow their trumpets in joy,
Not knowing the battalions you left to smote them.
Today, I lead the army to the front for you.
To fight the War 'of Bate Besong by Bate Besong'

No More DISGRACE, your last words.

Ripples of a Tide: A Time to Mourn
Katakata

The tide ripples at the foot of the mountain:
a breathe went out at low ebb,
when the first streaks of daylight hadn't yet found
the canopies of the evergreen forest.
Even so, the timber lorry, laden
with the legs of the firmament,
already ploughing its way to the wharf
without fog lights.
A tide ripples at the foot of the mountain:
and the blood that is spilled,
shall plug fear into every hole on the banks of the river,
that the sleeping earth will heave with spite.
Death has come to roost.
And the fierce plumeless-necked cockerel lies stilled,
its wing-bones no more than
the mishmash of our gory highways.
There was a time for us to chatter
and bask in the shade of its wings and stride.
All that's no more.
And if you don't know, Lorenzio,
I talk about the dead and the nightmare
that's our inheritance.
It's a time to mourn the colony.

On My Dying
(A Poem Bate Besong Would Write Now)
Christmas Ebini

I leave you
With no regrets
As I see the porter
Of the beautiful gates
A broad smile
On his face
With a bunch of keys
In his broad hands

He is getting ready
To open the bright gate
As I stand looking
Wondering my new fate

Then he looks at me
A look of invitation
This way he says
Through this gate of life
The saints are waiting
On my early coming
And everything is set
For my new christening.
As I leave you
Weep not my departure
For I filled my page
Of the struggle for justice

As I leave you today
Just as I came yesterday
With nothing to leave behind
But the footprints of a struggle

I see those who left earlier
Curious to know how you are
If injustice still exists
As they left behind

I tell them of your struggle
Against the strong forces of evil

That manufacture fear and hate
Against you and your children

As you stay lively behind
Do not give in to the devil
For his forces were long destroyed
Though he pretends to intimidate

Keep on the good fight
For sweet justice and freedom
Till the day your time comes
To join me to fight no more

Inextinguishable Flame... Timeless Spirit
Kangsen Feka Wakai

Death: a cruel but inevitable transition
Let your blood be libation to the gods
For the sanctification of a benighted nation
Your words are engraved
On the impenetrable caves of eternity
Yours is a timeless echo
That will forever ignite earthquakes
In our consciousness
You:
Patron saint of impassive bards
You:
Medium of clarity-agent of restless ancestors
You:
Pristine conscience of a fragile land
You:
Doughty mercenary of primordial origins
You:
Obasinjom Warrior-spirit in flesh
You:
Genius!
Timeless two-legged sphinx
Your cameo in this tragicomedy
Of ours is not over!
Yours is an eternal song
BB on the mic
Francis Bebey playing Fela's horn
Mongo Beti on drums...the gods are clanging their gongs
You:
Molyko's inextinguishable flame
Singing cantatas and with Okigbo
Scribbling post-modernist epistles with U-Tam'si
You:
Immortal louse inhabiting the bushy hair strands
Of accursed demagogues [our leaders]
They'll forever be sleepless
Your words are a terminal virus
In the shit-filled entrails of these humanoid vultures
BB
Lone pearl in a mound of coarse granite
Your sparkle will forever illuminate us

You:
Volcano of a spirit
Voice of protest
Voice of reason
Voice of hope
You:
Son, brother, father, husband, poet
You:
Teacher, playwright, scholar, critic, muse
You:
Artist, rebel, writer, mentor, friend...
Mind over matter...spirit over flesh...mind over matter...BB lives
forever
You:
Inextinguishable flame...timeless spirit

... Rest softly
Kenn Wanaku

How does one write an eulogy for friends/brothers
prematurely and roughly harvested from the garden of life,
when one can still taste the salt from one's tears?
BB, Gwangwa'a, Ambe and Awoh ...
in one fell swoop, your souls were made to exit
without any formality from this physical plane.
As the winds blow over Mount Fako
And the rains in Debundscha fill up all the
potholes of our motherland with promise
of fertility and good harvest,
As the thunder strikes
And the lightning lights up the skies
Let you all vent out the anger and pain
that your brutal coda would have built up.
When the ray of sunlight breaks open
the thick clouds above our ancestral lands,
Your spirits should know the peace that
all your loved ones pray that you have.
Rest brothers.

The Ascent
Babila Mutia

I
A Caravan of white buffalos
Echoes your name
On golden summits of
Phosphorus glowing mountains

& your spirit is trapped in mangled metal
On the road to Edea, not yet ascended.

Twelve candle stands
& glowing balustrades
Of sanctifying incense witness
This apparition of
Monks from gothic monasteries
Heads bowed in prostration
To the endless columns of
These cherubim and seraphim

& your spirit is still earthbound,
Not yet ascended.

For unto us a warrior was delivered
& from us a prophet has been taken.
Distant drumbeats
Herald his transformation
& the Obasinjom dancers
Sway in hypnotic frenzy

& your spirit staggers on the road to Edea
Still earthbound.

II
St. Patrick's Catholic Church,
Close to the University of Buea:
Choirboys in robes of alabaster
Join the hallelujah chorus
In joyous epiphany,
Arpeggio of D in the middle octave
& diatonic of scales above

& your spirit vibrates in indecision,
Not yet ascended.

Gigantic pipe organs grind
Away the warrior's laments
To scalp-raising crescendos
As ripples of celestial waves
Break & recede endlessly
On shingles & pebbles
On islands unknown
In pinnacles of cosmic shores

& your spirit vibrates,
Vibrates in uncertainty.

III
& behold the glorious
Miracle of Pentecost:
In one mighty surge of
Iridescent illumination
Vibrating spectrums of
Resurrection fires blind
Feeble mortal eyes

& your spirit vibrates
The spirit vibrates.

Ten thousand harpsichords
Double the soprano on D minor
With trumpets & trombones.

& your spirit ascends
The spirit is lifted up
Leaving behind the
Pathos of ephemeral mortality
To be received in immortality
& crowned in the
Cathedral of saints.

BB, You Must Have Known
Victor Epie'Ngome

BB, you must have known
That the requiem was at hand -
Yours before the Kaiser's -
So you sang with haste
Both psalm and antiphon
While the congregation yawned
Which now sings *dies irae*
You must have sensed your parting
With this material world
And so set your heart
Above its gossamer trappings
And upon the imperishable
It will echo on
Your laugh of derision
At them whose illusory living
Is but bare existence -
Belching opulence notwithstanding
It will reverberate till tomorrow
The loud report
Of your Kalashnikov voice
Rattling home hard truths
To ears that that would fain be lulled
With blandishment and platitudes
You go in the flesh -
T'was but a matter of time -
But you stay in the spirit
Of your shared knowledge -
Your enduring wealth
In a lifetime of deprivation
Death, thou art disgraced.
The Obasinjom warrior had long seen
Beyond your fearsome mask
And called your bluff

Beast on the Rampage
JK Bannavti

Bugle of the muzzled and lyre of the hurting fools
Milk of the starved and spring in the scourging noon
Path of the legless and staff of the blind
Machete of our fathers and warrior with the prize
Shower of Munchi Doga and grace of the hunchback
Pain of Ednouay and dread of Adinginging
Rain in his wedding and urine in his wine
Eye in his cupboard and fangs on his crimes
Reviled visitor, it is night
The beast is on rampage
Beast of no nation

"For what?" you ask
Aye, MY pound of flesh!
Who gave you knowledge?
Who showed you MY rituals?
Who showed you MY bedroom?
Who showed you MY mobile bank?
Who showed you MY harem of women?
Who showed you MY pillage of the hunchback?
Who showed you MY fleets, MY trips, MY flock, MY stars, MY moons?

You send night soil men to leave dung on MY red carpet
You let them foul the air right in front of YOUR revered chief
You let them break MY serenity with their HOARSE voices
You disturb MY lunch with the cries of hunchbackers
You refuse you bombed the Mungo bridge
You refuse you were caught red-handed
You gave munchi doga directions to Ednouay
My most holy Adinginging, creator of shrimps and crabs
Listen if you ever have ears
This one lying here is not me
I was gone before you showed up
Cut down all the shrubs on the walls of the Mountain
Divert the Mungo so it flows not through my heart
Clear the clouds over the kilum

Now gather all the first males in the hunchback
Blast their skulls for your noontime fun

Gather everything that gives birth in that land
Roast it alive to make sure all is gone
Smash the Chong and the Takumbeng
Burn the pumpkin
Break the calabash

Now turn around, you beast of no nation!
Do you see the desert you have created?
Are you satisfied?
Are you ready?
Now watch out for the rolling boulders
The dance of the mountains just started
They will soon vomit fire
Watch out for the spills of Nyos

Mon cher beast of no nation
See how shallow thou art?
Now you stumble and scamper
You mighty beast on rampage
At the sight of only one boulder
The dance only just started.

Adieu Bate Besong "BB" and Companions
Cyrille Kongnso

And yet departs another,
not alone but with some others.
The cold hands of death again,
with that dreadful sting without bargain.
The warrior amidst the warlords
singled and crushed as though were nothing.
What a shame that man as great,
nothing of him but wit bereft.
Wisdom and strength, power and reason,
all in him be found,
yet death his soul spareth n'er, tho his
earthly tast be-endeth nay.
Gone where so much they cherished be,
amongst the scholars their wit to share,
where politics and drama no more from their tongue doth sprout,
but thoughts of peace in the land beyond.
His epistles in us memory of him,
never from us shall depart, as all around centers
of learning thoughts of him shall relay.
Death so cruel took them both,
mentor and heir
where no heir as great as Kwasen
his master ever could replace.
Yet tho, the night by us so long shall remain
as we with them from this earthly world doth part.
Adieu BB and Co, Requiescat in Pace.

Farewell BB
Festus Akemfua

You knew too well the face of this day
These seasons that fed us with hunger and pain
You wailed out loud
As the cloak of darkness fell
As the chanting of the anthem fell out of rhythm
To the resonating sounds of the drums
You saw the scar- faced land, your land
And the knife sharp and stained with blood
You saw the desecration of the alter of Dreams
Your voice rose like thunder!

And we heard it
We heard it again and again
Hoping it will crack the sky
Hoping it will pierce the deafness of the false gods
Lording over the seven hills of Ednouay
And did it?
You could no longer stand the heat of the torturous season
The humiliation of an impoverished race-
As you fired on with your vexed tongue
Who did not think your lips will split off!

I hear silence as after an echo
Silence that soaks like cold rain
I stare into space with dried out eyes
Having wrestled fiercely with life
You could not succumb to death in one piece

You departed in cherished company
Swiftly taken from our midst
Having answered your call
You finished your work
You finished it well.

Bad Boy
Ekpe Inyang

Obasinjom warrior
Alias BB
Brave Boy
Bad Boy!?!
Tireless warrior

You intoned the tune
Of reformist chants
And charted the course
Of bad boys' march

Against inventors of notes
Completely out of tune
You preached apocalypse
And doom
Spat out venom
As weapons

Blasted ugly craft
To ensure the use
Of good notes
For composing sonnets and anthems
Of progress
How far did you go in the battle
How near are we to Completion Point
No answer
Brave lone warrior?

You crafted crown for your coronation
Platted with scales and spines and quills
Of reformist missiles

And then...
You vanished in four bloody jets
Too swift for my weak brain
To fathom
You're gone

To return
In multiple numbers

And manifold forms
With new craft
To conclude the battle?

Or
Was that your kind of stop
To the long, sweaty; tricky
And oft bloody battle?
Bad boy!

Bate Besong ajaoh!!

Joyce Ashuntantang

BB Ajaoh!! The Ekpe salutes
"Ooooo" the Obasinjom drools in spirit
To begin a search down here.
Your welcome on high
in tumultuous accolades
Reverberates in ripples below.
The crowd surged and drowned my tears
The Ekinni came but nothing could he steal
All I had was your ink
With that we'll smear them
With that we'll paint them
With that we'll build
Intricate patterns
For beautiful ones must be born
Born from your ink still dripping wet
BB ajaoh!!! Nfor Ngbe ekati ajaoh!!

A Tear For Bate Besong
Wache Henry Ndifon

All we can say is that
It's very hard to believe
But it is on that fateful day
That you met with your lot
When as some now whisper
You should have spent it to banquet
With your missus
As every macho was obliged to have done

But BB on your way out already
You were
Your co. K. Gwangwa'a and
H. Ambe were all with you at
Disgrace:
The last, the very last "outpouring of (your) spontaneous feelings
recollected" in nirvana
Though not Pax 'Nuoermak' didn't provide for that
Gone you are
But such as Marvin Gaye
Your elf lives on
The cruelest exit
Yours was:
Disgrace surely will
Flash the light in the very inner chambers of those whose
performance is a Disgrace
The remaining dregs of
'les anglofous' you have abandoned
Behind and in the jungle
"les freres "of your own very
Beasts of No Nation sigh in pessimism
Journey on well BB
To where there are no 'ribes
Nor 'rangling
Nor 'lamour
Nor 'cquisition
Illicit or not
You looked lost
In Pax Africana, in miniature
But it is in going
That you have yourself

Found
Oh! Douala-EDEA-Ednuoay
Alley
Our uni-gurus
You persevere
To yank; intermittently
Mellow, intermittently not
From Prof. Obenson to Gabriel Nlep
Onto Bate Besong, Gwangwa'a and Ambe
Oh expiration!
Be not spirited
For we expire
Only to subsist
So 'earth be not Chesty

Requiem for the Genuine Intellectual
Peter Vakunta

He's not here;
yet far and away
echoes of his prolific
erudition resounds.
He's not here;
but the legacy of his
intellect lives here.
He's not here;
but rumblings of his
cantankerous castigation
of an inept system clamors.
He's is not here;
still far and wide
the melody of his vociferation
against a cancerous polity chimes.
Hail BB!
The genuine intellectual,
The man who relegated
phony intellectualism,
professorship without publication
to the trashcan of academe.
BB is dead
Long live BB!
Who is immortal?
Big or small,
Rich or poor,
Corruptible or incorruptible,
Miscreant or holier-than-thou,
All food for maggots!

Flowing Like a Stream
Ekpe Inyang

Materials
as building blocks
to make
the message crystal-clear
and safe for public consumption
must flow like a stream

Those at the rear
may take their place at centre stage
or rank themselves with leaders high because
it must flow like a stream

Those at the fore-ranks
may choose
to bring up the rear
or take their place at centre stage because
it must flow like a stream
Those at the centre
may tail the crowd as hand-clappers
or join the ranks of leaders tall because
it must flow like a stream

Centre
rear or front or where
won't name you goat or dog or pig
or whatever
won't bring you frontal headache
backache
stomach-ache
toothache
if where you are is insurance that
it will flow like a stream

Multifaceted BB
Anne Tanyi -Tang

Obasinjom Warrior
Soyinka of Manyu
Modern Socrates
Weapon to man's conscience

A Prophet who saw what others could not see
A fighter for the downtrodden
A marvel of the brain
Millenarianist...

Like all great teachers and philosophers
Doomed to have a short life
Yet a life pregnant with purpose and meaning
Like all great teachers and philosophers
Destined to face the bloodiest and most cruel death

Death, the supreme healer
Has taken you to the world beyond
To meet your maker
You were a rare species
That visits once in a millennium
Neither understood nor accepted by this world...

Farewell irreplaceable sweet Prince
Salute Homer, Aeschylus, Sophocles, Euripides,
Socrates, Virgil, Milton, Shakespeare, Sankara,
Biko, MLK, and a host of your own kind.

* The paper that Bate Besong was supposed to present at the Association of African Literature (ALA) conference in Morgantown, USA, was titled "Anne Tanyi Tang's Socio-Political Satires: Retrogression and Resistance in Cameroon Drama".

Quo Fata Vocant: Where The Fates Call
Poubom Lamy Ney

I
The fates are not retired
Never do they get tired
Clotho encore spins the thread of life
Lachesis still determines its length
Atropos atrociously always cuts it off
And shouts loud A DIEU

II
Even the Nkpe have heard
That B.B has changed Waka in Sawa land
Leaving behind words as miraculous weapons
Orphaned

III
So are they wailing by the unknown wall:
The last supper as book launch
Was a launch with death dessert
Served on the road
For an out-of-earth journey

I can see the trap-like saucer
Deep with seeds of sorrow
For tears over years in fear
And its icy contents of broken lives
As cold as non-life and food for thought
In a glassy car mirroring corpses

If twins are born together
Who would name who die together
Coining the word and their world
Is no more

Say Bate the Bee-song
His honey was more than money
Sugaring the literary coffee
Of all who wish to break the fast

He has left no chance for Ambe
To stage his Disgrace with grace

And far none for Kwasen
To ever reintroduce him in banquets

IV
The zombies are now freer
To read
To bear cruel death as their title
They laugh like beasts of no nation
Who still will denounce their misdeeds
And pronounce and announce their disgrace
When in public Grace-the-country weeps
For being undressed without dowry
For being raped

The Obscure Intellectual Lives On
Stephen Neba-Fuh

Speak not,
Except your voice enriches
Silence's tranquility.

Write not,
Except your ink isn't to soil
The fine works of pulp's craftsmen.

Read not,
Except your prejudices aren't buried
In your mind's contours.

Listen not,
except you worry not of what
May not please your soul's audience.

Dr Jacobs BB lengthens the struggle,
By shortening the fear;
when contemporaries sit on the fence.

He listens, reads,
Writes and speaks.
The obscure intellectual lives on.

Adieu Prof!

Wache Henry Ndifon

Ah! BB ruined Nooremac's Literary guru
In a hodgepodge
Ever we are!!!
Like Shakespeare's Desdemona, BB
Nothing became Yours
Like the leaving of It

Lost though, your military and
unceasing
Spirit coruscates and thrives on.

Yours was of the spirit
Not the tissue

Fear, Force and Fraud
Our Lot and Trinity
You bagged
But forget not: the muggy terrain, you
know, persists, so your moxie we need.
Adieu anew Prof.

Death, Death and Death
E. E. Tayong

You go for the brave and courageous

leaving the weaklings and frivolous

You go for the substance leaving the shadow

You go for the heroes leaving the cowards

You go for the giants leaving the dwarfs.

But rest assured

One man has conquered you

We fall behind him

 We too shall conquer you.

Immortal Intellectual
(A Tribute to an Intellectual Scholar)
Ernest L. Molua

Your Flower Sprung in Cameroon
Your Narcissus Sprung in all Seasons
You Stood Intellectually Tall
You Left Your Prints on foothills of Mt Fako

BB, In Spirit Your Ink Still Flows
You are Immortal
Your Scholarship's Immortal
Tonight You are in God's Library
Ravaging Through Jesus' Books
Under the Watchful Eyes of Angels
Your Reading Lamp Shines Down on Cameroon

It is time to sleep, Sleep BB, gentle Sleep
Let Your work spring with beautiful flowers
The flowers of a Narcissus
Exceptional in the Tropics
Farewell, Compatriot.

A rare GEM
Stephen Neba Fuh

He spoke when everyone was expected to be silent.

He ran when everyone was admonished to walk.

He laughed when it was dangerous to be heard.

He crowed when others insisted it wasn't yet dawn.

He thought while the sages slept.

He wept while others laughed in ignorance.

He published, never to perish.

Because you did not Chop People Dem Money
Dibussi Tande

I

If only you had Chop People Dem Money
You would have traveled on the highway of death
In the safety of your own chauffeur-driven Prado
If only you had Chop People Dem Money
You would have had enough "awoof" vouchers
To purchase a thousand air tickets to Ongola
If only you had Chop People Dem Money
You would have had Uncle Sam's entry pass
Hand-delivered at your doorstep

But you refused to join the Kaiser and his courtiers
Who plunder the land with impunity
You chose the side of the people
And said "No!" to the evil cabal

If only you had Chop People Dem Money
You would still be with us in flesh
But you would have been a lost soul
Silenced and emasculated,
Compromised and zombified;
So you lived on your own terms to your dying day.
And for that you have gained immortality.

II
They may dance with joy at Mvomeka'a
As you lie in state in Ndekwai
But you shall have the last laugh
For theirs is a dance of delusion
A third rate conjurer's bag of illusions
One day their champagne party will end
And they'll end up where they rightfully belong
In the dustbin of history –
Mere meteors in the dark skies
Fizzling into oblivion…

III
You sang to your own tune
And danced to your own beat;
You played your part

And paid your dues;

The curtain has fallen
You've taken your final bow
And exited the stage
As the crowd begs for an encore
Vintage BB to the very end!!!

Farewell dear friend
Farewell teacher
Farewell great bard
Farewell freedom fighter

Thank God you did not **C**hop **P**eople **D**em **M**oney!!!

They are Gone!
Katakata

They are gone!
Okokobioko scholars
Can now take the stage
Let the drums roll
Let the dance begin
Let mediocrity reign.

Postscript

Bate Besong or the Symbol of the Cameroon Divide

"And yet, there was a time when people had faith, implicit faith - in this Union – without making any investigations. But I ask you, where is that faith now? It has vanished. So utterly! The bonds have snapped. We carry the scars of 'brotherhood' in a country so unaccustomed to candour." *Bate Besong, 1993.*

A common (in fact the most prevalent) theme in Bate Besong's writings (fiction and non-fiction) is the fate of Cameroon's English-speaking minority whom he referred to in his famous *Beasts of No Nation* as 'nightsoilmen" locked up in the antechamber of the republic; a people whose culture, history and even existence was an afterthought to the French-speaking majority of the bilingual Cameroon Republic. BB strongly believed that the unification of the British Southern Cameroons and the French Cameroons in 1961 was an unmitigated disaster for the Southern Cameroonians; that rather than giving birth to a new rainbow nation that took great pride in its diversity, the union had created a state built on deceit, and the exploitation and marginalization of Southern Cameroons. As BB lamented in his legendary keynote address at the Goethe Institute in 1993:

"… after lunatic route we took from Foumban, as in a Dantean Inferno, the Anglophone Cameroonian occupies the center of Hell. The surrounding concentric rings of this smouldering infernal canyon may embrace a multitude of other victims in the present Cameroonian reality, but there is no doubt that our people, subjected to perpetual mental and psychological servitude, are the story book victims of a cultural holocaust. History has since the biblical Cain and Abel – carved no grimmer monuments to its own propensity for unfathomable cynicism and evil.

In many quarters BB was described as unpatriotic and radical because of his uncompromising stance on the Anglophone problem in Cameroon. But that did not bother him one bit. As he responded tongue-in-cheek to a question about his patriotism and nationalism in 1992: "I can sell Cameroon for less than Asoumou's whisky. So I will not say I am a nationalist as such, for, I am definitely a patriot of Southern Cameroons, not *La Republique.*

But being a Southern Cameroons "patriot" did not mean blindly following or uncritically embracing the sometimes suspect leadership and dogma of the plethora of Southern Cameroons "liberation movements" that sprang up in the past decade. In this regard, his merciless flaying of the SCNC leadership back in 2000 (*The Post*, No. 155, Monday, January 24, 2000) which "gave no leadership, clarified nothing, and confused everything" was one for the history books:

> We, Southern Cameroonians, have always had leaders that are archetypal mediocres: tribalistic, deceitful and fraudulent - since Foumban. Our daily lives are, therefore, viewed by the neo-colonial askari, through a distorted Quai d'Orsay prism, where the sum total of a person's character, merit, and worth is defined by De Gaulle's language. We have always been frog-marched in the limbo of marginality, alienated and directionless. In the depths of ignominy.

As far as BB was concerned, the bilingual Cameroon republic was a state made up of two nations, and that the country's curse was its continued refusal to come to terms with this reality, which no amount of state-decreed "national integration" could ever erase.

Even in his death, Bate Besong – that vocal symbol of Anglophone alienation - was still able to prove his point that national integration was a sham whose ultimate goal was to make English speaking Cameroonians invincible and irrelevant. Today, March 21, 2007, some two weeks after the three prominent Cameroonian men of arts - BB, Hilarious Ambe and Kwansen Gwangwa'a - perished in that horrific accident in Misole II, not one leading French language newspaper has devoted a single line to their death. Even the fact that with their death, the University of Buea has lost a record eight lecturers within a year, and the country, one of its leading TV and Film directors, has not been enough to interest the French language tabloids – even as a purely human interest story...

That Bate Besong, the award-winning literary colossus whom critics labeled the "Cameroonian Soyinka" or the "Anglophone Mongo Beti" died and folks "on the other side of the bridge" – as he euphemistically referred to Francophones – did not notice, would surprise many non-Cameroonians. Especially those in African literature circles. However, this would not come as a surprise to BB at all. In fact, I can see him in my mind's eye laughing sarcastically with an I-told-you-so look on his face. As he pointed out in numerous articles, post independent Cameroonian literature has been characterized by a systematic disdain, marginalization, neglect, and non-recognition of the works by English-speaking Cameroonians – a point that Edward Ako (2004, 57) grudgingly conceded:

> If it is true that there can be no meaningful discussion of African literature without reference to such Cameroonian authors as

Mongo Beti, Ferdinand Oyono, Rene Philombe, Calixte Beyala and Guillaume Oyono Mbia, it is also true that such discussions never include authors writing in English.

In "New Engagements in Cameroonian Literature: the Other Side of the Bridge", BB, however, reminded Francophone literary critics that the "literature of the Hunchback" from west of the River Mungo had nothing to envy qualitatively from the literature from the other side of the bridge:

On the Cameroonian muses' crowded pantheon therefore, we too have been firm of feet as your own Fabien Eboussi Boulaga, Guillaume Oyono Mbia, Charly Gabriel Mbock, Gaston Paul Effa, Jacques Fame Ndongo, Hubert Mono Ndjana, Ferdinand Leopold Oyono, the immortal Mongo Beti. (But, ignorance, as Plato remarked, is at the root of most misfortunes).

The official discourse in Cameroon may propagate the myth of "oneness"; the fairytale of one people and one nation under God living happily ever after, but BB knew better and said it loud and clear: There are TWO Cameroons, with two very different and sometime diametrically opposed histories and cultures; two Cameroons with two different sets of socio-political and literary icons – strangers in the night walking past each other and barely saying Hello.

This explains why in 1990, for example, a special edition of the French language *Le Messager* newspaper which profiled dozens of "real heroes" of Cameroonian independence and reunification, did not mention a single citizen of the former British Southern Cameroons – not even those who helped keep the flame of the nationalist UPC burning after it was banned in the French Cameroons. Or those Southern Cameroonians who in 1961 rejected the Nigerian option against all odds to throw in their lot with the alien and French-speaking *La Republique du Cameroun* in the name of the *Kamerun Idea*.

In an October 1998 discussion on the CAMNET internet forum about the systemic Francophone disdain for everything Anglophone, particularly its history, Steve Andoseh wrote:

What is clear is that the propensity for Francophones to ignore Anglophone Cameroon history reflects the systemic marginalization of Anglophone Cameroon by the majority. The fact that it goes almost unperceived by them only proves how endemic the problem is.

This exercise in the appropriation of history - replete with complete discretion over its revision upon the authority of the narrator being of or from whence such history emanates - is what passes for education of our people on our history. Even the events currently unfolding under our very eyes are distorted unscrupulously by those who think they have the moral authority to do so - who think they have some right to determine what is truth.

It is as a result of a similar appropriation of Cameroonian literature by those on the other side of the bridge that the Bate Besongs, the Hansel Ndumbe Eyohs or the Kenjo Jumbams can be considered – oh sacrilege! – literary nonentities in Cameroon. And, it is this appropriation which has given birth to that lopsided "narrative" in which Bate Besong the literary giant never existed and therefore never died – hence the silence of the Francophone media. BB can feature prominently in the *Encyclopedia of African Literature* along greats such as Soyinka, Achebe, Ngugi, Coetzee, etc. but he definitely has no place in an *Encyclopédie de la littérature camerounaise* alongside Calixte Beyala and others from the other side of the bridge.

Again, BB would be totally unfazed by the preceding observation. Which is why he did not believe that the writer west of the Mungo divide should waste time, resources and energy trying to gain access into a mythical Francophone-controlled Cameroonian literary pantheon. Instead, he saw the Anglophone writer as a revolutionary activist busy documenting and echoing the plight of his people. As he argued ferociously back in 1993:

> The Anglophone Cameroonian Writer must never forget his origins. His writing must depict the conditions of his people, expressing their spontaneous feeling of betrayal, protest and anger.
>
> It must challenge. It must indict head on. His writing must open up the Chinese Wall of Opportunity, closed to his people for over three decades.
>
> Our literature must convey with remarkable force the moods of the Anglophone Cameroonian caught in the assimilation-nightmare of Sisyphean existence. That literature must be inspired by an historical myth-informed consciousness. It must embody in bold relief the specific historical features of the entire Cameroonian reality.
>
> We must not evade the issues raised by economic, social and political change. We will be criticized for presenting the frustration and agony of a people held as a hostage minority. But we must insist on the truth of what we write. The Anglophone Cameroonian writer at home and in the Diaspora must tell the

outside world the story of his tragic land from the point of view of its hostage minority.

That determination to tell the story of his people no matter the personal and professional cost; to empower the people of the former British Southern Cameroons with the facts of their history and instill in them an unshakable pride in their own identity, is what simultaneously made BB "The symbol of Anglophone hope" (Ngwane, 1993) and the "symbol of the Cameroon Divide". He was a visionary who clearly understood the role of reconstituted memory in awakening the collective consciousness of his people being crushed under the weight of "feudal oppression, mountains of suspicions and hate, retrogression, post-Foumban pauperization [and] resentment". As he opined in his piece on E.T Egbe (2005) "Memory will remain an important talking drum to the present on how the historical journey of a people is perceived, against the backdrop of an oppressive, neo-colonial culture."

In that landmark address at the Goethe Institute in 1993, Bate Besong hammered home the fact that:

No one can speak for us. Only those who daily live through the humiliations, the third class citizenship, in the abattoir of servitude, only we can fully comprehend and explore these contradictions in a society undergoing such rapid and confusing transition.

That is BB's ultimate message to the children of the former British Southern Cameroons: They may despise and ignore us on the other side of the Mungo bridge; they may trample on our history, our literature, our culture, our people and our heroes; but as long as we never stop singing "King Alpha's song in a strange land", the day of reckoning will eventually come to pass…

So a baobab fell in the forest and they refused to notice? We don't give a damn!!!!!!!!!!!!!!!

Farewell BB. See you on the other side.

Dibussi Tande
Chicago (USA)
March 21, 2008

References

Ako, Edward. (2004). "Nationalism in Recent Cameroon Anglophone Literature. In Marsden, P. H., & Davis, G. V. *Towards a transcultural future literature and human rights in a 'post'-colonial world.* ASNEL-papers, 8. Amsterdam: Rodopi.

Bate Besong. "The Fall of Sesekou E. T. Egbe and The Book of his Life". *The Post,* Friday, April 1, 2005.

_____. *New Engagements in Cameroon Literature: The Other Side of the Bridge,* 2004. www.batebesong.com

_____. "Esuka Ndoki's Quisling SCNC: After The Ekontang Elad Particular." *The Post* newspaper No. 155, Monday, January 24, 2000.

_____. (1993). "Literature in the Season of the Diaspora: Notes to the Anglophone Cameroonian Writer". In Lyonga, N., Breitinger, E., & Butake, B. *Anglophone Cameroon writing.* Bayreuth African studies series, 30. Bayreuth, Germany: Eckhard Breitinger.

Ngwane, George. (1993). *Bate Besong (or the symbol of Anglophone Hope.* Limbe: Nooremac Press.

I went, I saw, I did not Conquer

Yes, after writing poetry, crying, making and receiving frantic calls from and to Cameroon, it was clear that I had to go to the land of my birth to see for myself and be a witness not only to the dramatic exit of the erstwhile Obasinjom warrior, Emanyangkpe, iconoclast, playwright, poet, scholar, and social critic, Dr. Bate Besong , but also to witness the exit of the other two literary gurus, Television Producer, Thomas Kwasen Gwan'gwaa and Dr. Hilarious Ambe who died alongside BB.

I left the United States on the 14th of March 2007 and arrived the next day in Douala at night. After having a restless sleep, I left for Yaoundé the following morning, March 16th, and arrived just in time for the viewing of Victim number one, Thomas Kwasen Gwan'gwaa. After the funeral rites in Yaounde, I joined family and friends that night for another tedious five hour plus trip to Bali, Northwest Cameroon, for the burial. From Gwan'gwaa's burial, I rushed to Bafut on the same day to witness the burial of Victim number 2, Hilarious Ambe and the next day, I was back on the road to Yaoundé to prepare for my descent, and Yes, ascent to Buea to be a witness to the traumatic funeral ceremony of the now legendary Bate Besong.

March 21st 2007 was the D day. The crowd at the mortuary was over two thousand including both friends and foe. Buea had not seen any thing like that. BB had been such a public figure that he had become more of a symbol than a real person. But his death proved that he was just human, born of woman. And true, BB's mother was at the mortuary. I stared at her for sometime wondering: how does a woman raise a child who becomes a symbol of hope for a people? When does she realize that such a child will carry the burden of his people? How does a mother mourn a child who symbolized the anger of a people? How does a mother's personal grief negotiate the boundaries and margins of this show of public grief?

I moved from the mother to the wife. I took a hard look at Mrs. Christina Besong. I had condoled with her privately the night before but seeing her at this juncture in her white mourning outfit in public view brought up questions in my mind. What did she know that we didn't? In the course of knowing BB it was sometimes easy to forget that he had a family because he was usually engrossed in matters of national import. However, in a rare glimpse of carnal emotion BB wrote these lines for Christina in a poem of that same title:

Woman, your image, newly grained, season fevered
Revelations, too, where my ploughs have lain

Secretions tread Easter pods to lave
White havens, sweet-shawled in loin chambers.

I pondered this poem in my mind as I gazed at the woman, whose husband I had flown all the way to come and mourn. What role did she play in the several volumes of plays and collections of poetry that he produced? From what I knew of BB, I figured, Christina must have been the earth to which BB planted his feet, so he could hold steady his pen.

I looked at his children. Although his daughters were his scribes, it is in the naming of his male children that BB revealed his mind, from the oldest named Dante through his middle son, Mandela to his youngest son, Eldridge. Thus in-between the foremost Renaissance poet, Dante Alighieri, the revolutionary freedom fighter, Nelson Mandela to Eldridge Cleaver, the Black Panther activist writer, Bate Besong had forged his own identity, an identity which garnered him disciples as well as detractors.

As my mind surveyed BB's family at the mortuary I realized that I will leave Cameroon with more questions than answers. So by the time the convoy moved to the University of Buea for academic honors, my brain, mind and soul were playing ping-pong trying to decipher who in fact was BB in his totality.

My flight was that same day, so after presenting my eulogy to the mammoth crowd that had overflowed the Amphitheatre 750 at the University, I bowed in respect and awe in front of the casket carrying the remains of the enigmatic Obasinjom warrior. Yes I had flown to Cameroon for my grief to find succor but as I entered the car that was on standby to rush me to the airport, it was very clear that I came, I saw but did not conquer…and I now know why…BB's job is not yet done…his death is just another foundation for the builders left behind…*aluta continua*!

Joyce Ashuntantang
Storrs (USA)
January 17, 2008

Bate Besong on Bate Besong

My writing output as a whole (drama, poetry, theory) has received serious attention in book-length studies, journal articles, research papers, seminar presentations and theses and dissertations. Having been "stereotyped" by literary scholars and critics as the "outspoken dissident" and major author of the new literature of a democratic Cameroon, I would like to suggest that I have experimented with symbolic tableaux, dramatic illusion, mimicry and pageant elements to illuminate the theatrical drabness of the emergent Cameroon theatre since the turbulent nineties.

My political orientation (i.e. revolutionary socialism) has led me to experiment with both elements of African folk iconography and the Brechtian alienation techniques thereby balancing aesthetics against ideology to avoid outright propaganda.

Mine has therefore been a vision of writing as a vibrant social institution that must dare to be dangerous: irreverently iconoclastic, mocking, belligerent, even anarchistic, but essentially amiable.

My work is aggressively revolutionary, using imagistic patterns of symbolic imprimatur; dramatizing topical political issues, and thereby seeking to expose the corruption, oppression and incompetence of a post-colonial, prebendal, neo-colonial, power structure. My writing unites the macabre and the exuberant.

Dear Reader: I write satirically and passionately on artistic freedom, historical, social and political themes; on literary craft; on the harrowing stories of victims on the periphery of capitalist/tribal violence, and the widening circle of loss...

I am an inveterate experimenter with language and I love to challenge society's conventions regarding basic aspects of the Cameroonian condition.

For instance, my 1990 play *Beasts of no Nation* (a docu-drama) opened a new epoch of political protest theatre in Cameroon and went on, like *Requiem for the Last Kaiser,* to win international recognition as a dramatic model of revolutionary theatre.

I will always protest against injustices committed against the marginalized and bruised in the name of politics.

I will always deal with the internal conflict between forces of good and evil in settings borrowed from history and myth.

The End

www.batebesong.com
January 9, 2006

Glossary

Adinginging: Dictator. A term coined by Bate Besong in his most popular work, *Beasts of No Nation,* to describe Cameroon's Presidents.

Ajaoh! On the spot ululation of praise for a person to acknowledge a good deed.

Anglofous: Derogatory name for English speaking Cameroonians commonly referred to as "Anglophones".

Awoof: Something that is (given for) free.

Ayo me! A Kenyang language expression of regret equivalent to "Had I Known" or in this context "Oh! dear me".

Chop People Dem Money: A Pidgin English term literally meaning "Eat people's money". It is a popular reinterpretation of the acronym of the ruling *Cameroon People's Democratic Movement* implying that CPDM officials are prone to embezzling and misappropriating state funds.

Chong: A women's cult from the Nso Fondom in the Northwest province of Cameroon.

Ednuoay: An anagram for Yaounde, Cameroon's political capital. BB used this as the setting of *Beast of No Nation.*

Ekinni: The messenger of Ngbe or Ekpe society.

Ekinni Acwhingbe: Messenger from the Ngbe lodge.

Ekinni, Neko piti piti: Go softly Ekinni.

Ekpe: Also known as Ngbe amongst the Ejagham/Bayangi of Cameroon. It is a secret society (leopard Society) open only to men. In the past it was in charge of law and order in the community. Also called Nyangkpe or Nkpe.

Gwet bi kundè: War of Independence in the language of the Bassa ethnic group of Cameroon.

Hunchback: Refers to that part of the map of Cameroon which protrudes like a hunchback and which corresponds to the former British Southern Cameroons or "Anglophone Cameroon".

Hunchbackers: Anglophone Cameroonians.

Kabukabu: A Nigerian term to describe unlicensed taxis. They are usually used cars imported from Europe.

Kabukabu lecturers: Lecturers with little or no academic pedigree who are not interested in scholarship and critical thinking. See also: **Okokobioko scholars.**

Kilum: A Mountain range in Elak-Oku (Bui division) in the Northwest province of Cameroon.

Mbongo Chobi: The main dish of the Bassa consisting of fish with dark sauce.

Misole II: The little hamlet in Bassa land where BB and his colleagues died. This explains the numerous references to Bassa mythology and culture in this collection.

Mpodol: "The Prophet", as the Bassa referred to Ruben Um Nyobe, founder of the Camerounian nationalist party, the *Union des Populations du Cameroun* (UPC) which launched an armed insurrection against French colonialists in the 1950s.

Munchi Doga: Nightsoilmen. Council workers in the former Southern Cameroons / West Cameroon, reputed to come from the Munchi ethnic group in Nigeria, whose job was to dispose of buckets of feces collected from latrines. They were considered the lowest class in society. Bate Besong used this term in *Beasts of No Nation* as a metaphor for the status of the Anglophone minority in Cameroon.

Mungo bridge: The bridge that links the English and French-speaking regions of Cameroon. It is generally used as a symbol of the unity, or lack thereof, between the inhabitants of both territories.

Musong: Black magic portion popular among the Bassa.

Mvomeka'a: The birthplace of President Paul Biya of Cameroon.

Ndekwai: Bate Besong's birthplace.

Nfor Ngbe ekati ajaoh!! The learned Doctor of letters, I ululate in praise before you.

Ngog Lituba: The sacred and mythical Rock Cave, the natural and spiritual sanctuary of the Bassa people.

Nooremac: Anagram for Cameroon

Nyos: A crater lake in the Northwest province of Cameroon which emitted a toxic gas in August 21, 1986 killing 1,700 people who lived nearby.

Obasinjom: A traditional cult and masquerade that originated in the Cross River area of Cameroon and Nigeria reputed to identify witches and wizards, then stripping them of their evil powers. BB was a native of this region.

Obasinjom Warrior: Term of endearment used to describe BB because of his tenacity in the face of adversity. BB first used the term in *Obasinjom Warrior with Poems After Detention*, a collection of poems which he published in 1991.

Okokobioko: An Ibibio word for a type of mushroom that grows on fallen trees. Also known as Kokobioko.

Okokobioko scholars: A metaphor for university lecturers who climb up the ranks not through scholarship and merit, but through gossip, slander and "toeing the line" of the university administration and the regime in power.

Ongola: The original / indigenous name of Yaounde.

Prado: A mid-sized Toyota luxury Sports Utility Vehicle (sold in the US as the Lexus GX) which has become the leading status symbol for the nouveau riche in Cameroon.

Takumbeng: A traditional society from the Ngemba kingdom of Cameroon composed exclusively of post-menopausal women whose role is to redress wrongs in the community. It played a prominent political role in the Northwest province following the reinstitution of multipartyism in Cameroon.

UB: The acronym for the University of Buea.

About the Contributors

Christopher Fon Achobang, a stone sculptor, poet, translator and social critic living in Victoria, Cameroon. He is a poet laureate of the International Society of Poets in Maryland, USA and a former columnist for Eden Newspaper.

Mukwelle Akale, served as teacher and high school administrator in various high schools in Cameroon, particularly GBHS Bamenda, before moving to the United States. He now lives in Palo Alto, California.

Festus Akemfua, a former student of BB's residing in Douala, Cameroon.

Solomon Amabo, former student of BB's at the University of Buea. He is a journalist working with Equinoxe Radio and Television in Douala and the local correspondent for Eden newspaper.

Sarah Anyang, lecturer, Department of English, University of Yaounde 1, Yaounde, Cameroon.

Joyce Ashuntantang, Professor of English and African Literature at the University of Connecticut at Storrs (USA), and an Associate to the UNESCO Chair and Institute for comparative Human Rights at the University of Connecticut.

Joseph K. Bannavti, theatre actor, director, playwright and journalist living in New Jersey (USA). JK co-directed the famous production of BB's *Beast of No Nation* at the University of Yaounde in 1991. He recently published a play titled *The Reapers.*

Christmas Ebini, Cameroonian community activist, essayist and poet living in Washington, DC. He is the author of two poetry collections, *Partners in Prison* and *Echoes of Mount Mary.*

Valentine Gana, BB's former student at CPC Bali from 1982 to 1984. His first book of poetry and prose, *Passionate Pearls of Wisdom,* was published in 2005. He lives in Overland Park, Kansas (USA).

Ekpe Inyang, Cameroonian environmental theater activist. His celebrated plays include *Beware* and *Sacred Forest.*

Katakata, pseudonym of a former student of the University of Buea.

Alfred Kisubi, Ugandan-born poet, Professor of Human Services at the University of Wisconsin-Oshkosh (USA). He is the author of the poetry collection, *Time Winds.*

Cyrille Kongnso, poet and travel consultant residing in Cyprus whose poetry has been greatly influenced by BB.

Fr Tatah Mbuy, diocesan priest of the archdiocese of Bamenda, Cameroon. He is a research scholar, writer and literary critic.

Ba'bila Mutia, Professor of Literature, ENS, University of Yaounde 1, Cameroon. His best known published works include; *The Miracle, Whose Land,* and *Before this Time Yesterday.*

Ernest Molua, lecturer in Economics at the University of Buea, Cameroon. He is the Editor of *The Entrepreneur,* Cameroon's leading English language economic newspaper

Wache Henry Ndifon, an experimental poet who lives in Kumbo, Cameroon. His Master's thesis at the University of Yaounde focused partly on the message and medium in Bate Besong's *Beast of No Nation.*

Stephen Nebah-Fuh, a graduate of the University of Buea, he is a political and social critic who uses poetry to promote justice and basic human rights. He lives in Norway and will soon publish his first collection of poems.

Poubom Lamy Ney, language/literature teacher and cultural curator. His poems have appeared in numerous publications. He lives in Buea and was BB's colleague and friend.

Ilongo Fritz Ngale, poet, philosopher and novelist living in Yaounde. He is the author of the novel, *The Four Pillars of Time.*

Victor Epie Ngome, veteran Cameroonian journalist, poet and playwright. He is the author of the critically-acclaimed play, *What God Has Put Asunder.*

Dibussi Tande, poet, essayist and journalist currently living in Chicago, USA. His poems have appeared in several anthologies and he recently published his first collection of poems titled *No Turning Back.*

Anne Tanyi-Tang, playwright, Senior Lecturer in the Department of Arts and Archaeology, University of Yaounde. Her published plays include *Ewa and Other plays* and *Enita vs Elimo.*

E. E. Tayong, a graduate of the University of Buea. He is a Thermo-Mechanical Engineer currently living in Copenhagen, Denmark.

Peter W. Vakunta, a doctoral student and teacher at the University of Wisconsin-Madison (USA). His fiction has appeared in numerous anthologies. His most recent publication is a collection of short stories titled *Grassfields Stories from Cameroon.*

Kangsen Wakai, poet, performance artist and writer based in Houston, Texas (USA). He has published two poetry collections, *Asphalt Effect* and *Fragmented Melodies.*

Kenn Wanaku, singer, songwriter and composer, and BB's schoolmate in St. Bede's College, Ashing-Kom (Cameroon). Kenn now lives in Maplewood, Minnesota (USA). His last album, *AfrikanGuitarStrophy,* received widespread acclaim.

Special Mention

Abidemi Olowonira, Nigerian-born visual artist, photographer and musician. His painting, "A Tribute to Bate Besong", graces the cover of this collection and was on exhibition at the Museum of Fine Arts in Houston (USA) in February 2008. He is completing a degree in Fine Arts at Texas Southern University in Houston. Abidemi's work has been exhibited in many local galleries and museums.

Bate Besong, a Select Bibliography

Selected Plays and Poetry Collections

2007. *Disgrace (Autobiographical Narcissus) & Emanya-Kpe* (*Collected Poems*). Limbe, Cameroon: Design House. 122 p.

2003. *Three Plays (The Achwümgbe Trilogy).* Yaounde , Cameroun: Editions CLE. 231 p.

2001. *Change Waka & His Man Sawa Boy.* Yaounde , Cameroon: Editions CLE. 65 p.

1998. *Just Above Cameroon (Selected poems 1980-1994).* Limbe, Cameroon: Pressbook. 34 p.

1997. *The Grain of Bobe Ngom Jua (Poems).* Bellingham, USA: Kola Tree Press. 40 p.

1994. *The Banquet. A Historical Drama.* Makurdi, Nigeria: Editions Ehi. 52 p.

1991. *Obasinjom Warrior with Poems after Detention.* Limbe, Cameroon: Alfresco. 43 p.

1991. *Requiem for the Last Kaiser (a drama of conscientization and revolution).* Nigeria: Centaur. 71 p.

1990. *Beasts of no Nation. A docu-drama.* Limbe, Cameroon: Nooremac Press. 52 p.

1986. *The Most Cruel Death of the Talkative Zombie. A faery play in three parts with a revelry at a requiem.* Limbe, Cameroon: Nooremac Press. 80 p.

1980. *Polyphemus Detainee & Other Skulls (poems).* Ibadan, Nigeria: Scholars Press. 44 p.

Selected Critical Works

2007. "The Failure of the Modern Aesop in Anglophone Cameroonian Drama: The Example of Hansel Ndumbe Eyoh's The Inheritance". *Journal of Third World Studies.* Vol. XXIV, No. 1, Spring.

2007. "Nationhood in Dramaturgy: Marginality and Commitment in Victor Epie Ngome's 'What God has Put Asunder'". In Pierre Fandio & Mondi Madini (eds). *Figures de l'histoire et imaginaire au*

Cameroun / Actors of history and artistic creativity in Cameroon. Etudes africaines. Paris, Harmattan.

2002. "Ontogenesis of Modern Anglophone Cameroon Drama and its Criticism: Excursus". *VOICES: The Wisconsin Review of African Languages and Literatures*. University of Wisconsin, Vol. 1 No. 5 1-19.

2002. "L'écrivain est mort: Alas, Poor Ferdinand (Son Excellence Leopold Oyono)" *ALA Bulletin*. Vol. 28, No. 2 Spring 119-124.

2001. "The Limits of a Manichean Vision and the Egoist Hero in Post Colonial Bourgeois Theatre". *Epasa Moto: A Bilingual Journal of Language and Literatures*. University of Buea. Vol. 1. No. 479 – 98.

1997. "Who's Afraid of Anglophone Theatre "I & II". *West Africa*, 7 – 3 July, pp. 1106 – 1107 & 14-20 July, p. 1146.

1993. "Literature in the Season of the Diaspora: Notes to the Anglophone Cameroonian Writer". In Nalova Lyonga, Bole Butake, Eckhard Breitinger (eds) *Anglophone Cameroon Writing*. Bayreuth: Germany. 5 – 18.

Interviews

2004. Fandio, Pierre. "Anglophone Cameroon Literature at Crossroads: Pierre Fandio in Conversation with Cameroonian Writer, Bate Besong". *ALA Bulletin*. Vol.30, No.2 Fall 2004/ No.3 Winter 2005. 90-104.

2004. Fandio, Pierre. « La littérature anglophone camerounaise à la croisée des chemins », entrevue avec Bate Besong. *Africultures*. No. 60.

2001. Bate Besong: "Why Literature does not Thrive in Cameroon". With Prof. Okome Onookome. *Daily Times of Nigeria*, 5 December.